THE
Last
EIGHT

THE
Last
EIGHT

Sharon Laupp

xulon press

Xulon Press
2301 Lucien Way #415
Maitland, FL 32751
407.339.4217
www.xulonpress.com

Paperback ISBN-13: 978-1-66282-810-2
Ebook ISBN-13: 978-1-66282-811-9

For Tom with love

ACKNOWLEDGMENTS

$\mathcal{T}$his trip and story could not have been written without my husband's continuous involvement. I am so thankful he liked my Christmas gift to him in 1995. Abigail would not be "alive" without his constant tinkering and care. His account of "Restoring Abigail" provided precise details of the many steps necessary to bring Abigail to achieve so many accomplishments. Tom provided countess tips and suggestions in the writing of this book.

Thanks to my lifelong friend Joan Alexander Vaughters for planting the seed in my mind to write a book about the trip. Also, thanks go to my friends Steve Brigham and Rebecca Sandlin for proofreading the manuscript before it was submitted to Salem Press. Janet Harshbarger, a fellow author from Andrews, provided valuable guidance and encouragement in the writing of this book. Thanks to my local librarians Nancy Disbrow and Dee Kochensparger, who made recommendations for me to navigate the writing and publishing of my book. The staff of Salem Press, especially Jesse Kegg and Bridget Ferrara and the editing, production and marketing staff are greatly appreciated.

To all the readers of *The Last Eight*, thank you. Hope you enjoyed the journey.

FALL 1995

---

*T*his saga began in 1995 when one Saturday after-noon in early September, my husband Tom and I decided to go to Auburn, Indiana, to the Auburn-Cord-Duesenberg festival. This Labor Day weekend annual event has something for everyone. Tourists from around the world mecca to Auburn, Indiana, to experience the Parade of Classics (Auburn-Cord-Duesenberg), the Hoosier Tour, the Auburn Auctions at both Worldwide Auctioneers and RM Auctions, swap meets, music, food, and fun. The festival's mission is to celebrate and pro-mote automobile heritage. We did not have any inten-tion to purchase anything except food but did take some checks with us "just in case." While there, we saw two cars that "spoke" to both of us—a 1930 Chevy coupe and a 1930 pickup truck. We liked the colors and general look of the vehicles. Both vehicles had the same owner and were set to auction the following Monday or could be purchased prior for $12,000 each. No way would that happen—too expensive—so we looked at more choices, had a bite to eat, and then headed home.

Two months later in November 1995, I was on my way to Christmas shop in Fort Wayne, Indiana, about forty miles from our home. On my way there, I saw an old car parked in the front yard of a home with a for sale sign in the windshield. That old car was a 1930 Tudor Model A Ford. I thought to myself, *I wonder if Tom would like that?*

Although Tom says we were looking at 1930 cars when we went to Auburn, I thought we were settling for a '50s or '60s car. So, I decided, "No, not that car." I proceeded forward on my trip for another fifteen miles. Then, I suddenly had the thought, *Maybe that car would work. No harm to at least look.*

I went back and decided to find out the details. A sign was posted in the car with contact information. I was disappointed that the car did not belong to the homeowners where the car was parked. I had been hoping to just go up to the door and speak with someone about the car but that did not happen. The only thing I could do was call the number listed on the sign. So, I said to myself, "Just finish your shopping trip." I got back on the road to Fort Wayne, but my inner voice said, "No, turn around. Go home and call that number!" This was a time before many people had cell phones and still had to depend on their home landlines. It is so much easier today with our ever-present cell phones. When I returned home, I called the number and spoke with the car owner's son, Don Jr., who was handling the details for his father, Don Sr. We spoke at length about the car, me asking, "Does it run? How much is it? When do you need my decision?" The answers were, "Yes, she runs; the cost is $4,500; and an answer as soon as possible."

CHRISTMAS 1995

---

*O*kay, I had some work to do. I did not have an extra $4,500 and did not want to take it out of our joint account. I walked into my bank and asked to speak with someone about a loan. It ended up being easy to get. The loan was in my name because the car was going to be a surprise Christmas gift for Tom. With the money in hand, I met Don Jr., purchased the car, and planned for it to stay in Don Jr.'s garage until Christmas Eve. Don Jr. would deliver the car to my neighbor Jim sometime before Christmas. On Christmas Eve, while we were at midnight Mass, Jim would drive the car to our garage. Then, when we came home, the surprise would be there.

Well, the day came, and things did not go as expected. Good thing Jim and I made an alternative plan because it looked like we were going to need it. My mother, Jessie, was visiting us for the holidays. She was in on the plan, and when the garage door opened, no car sat inside! She cast me a worried glance. My mother and I needed to act normally as if nothing were wrong, or Tom would know something was up. So, off to bed we went and waited for the alternative plan to fall into place.

Christmas morning arrived right on schedule. We had breakfast and waited for our daughter, Dawn, and her one-month-old son, Jaron, to arrive. They eventually got to our home, and we were about to open the presents when the phone rang. Tom answered it and immediately said, "Have to go across the street to Jim's. He has a problem." Well, I knew what kind of problem Jim had—he had Tom's car stuck in his garage! The four of us—my mom, daughter, grandson Jaron, and myself—waited a few minutes. Then we donned our winter coats and got in my car and drove to Jim's. We live in the country, and our neighbors are down the road a farm field away.

When we arrived at Jim's, he and Tom were standing in the driveway talking. The garage door was down, and Tom later said, "I wondered why Jim was just standing there and not showing me what his problem was!" Tom says that when he saw us coming, he realized something was up. We got out of the car just as Jim was opening the garage door to reveal a car covered by a tan cover and huge red bow. Tom took the car cover off, and his expression was worth all the effort made to get and hide the car. Jim said he had tried several times and could not get it started. When Tom got into the car, she started right up as if she knew Tom was "her new fella," and she behaved perfectly. Tom drove that little black car right home. Its first passengers were my mom, daughter, and grandson. I drove my car back home, and the celebration and story of Abigail was now in the Laupp family heritage.

When we left our neighbor's home, we headed south to our driveway. Tom hit the brakes to slow down for the left turn, and the car automatically turned left. The left brake was the only brake working, so the first project would need to be the brakes.

Tom driving Abigail home Christmas Day 1995.

RESTORING ABIGAIL

Tom writes:

After we got Abigail, I called the Indiana Motor Vehicle department and was able to trace the car back to its second owner through the registration information provided. From there, I found out who the first owner was. So here it goes.

John Adams of Canton, Illinois, bought the car in 1930 from the Fairview Ford dealership for $499. When Mr. Adams died, his wife put the car in the barn to rest for thirty years. She held an auction in 1972, and Mr. Richard Payne, also of Canton, bought the car. Unfortunately, in those thirty years of being in the barn, chickens, mice, racoons, and other critters had torn up the interior of the car. Mr. Payne installed orange corduroy in all the interior, seats, ceiling, and side panels. You can see some of the orange corduroy in the grinder picture. I took all the orange out as soon as I started working on the car. I would have loved to have had the fog light pictured in the "in the barn" picture, but it was long gone.

Abigail after thirty years in the barn.

Richard Payne and his son grinding sausage using the real wheel of Abigail.

The picture of the wheel meat grinder shows Mr. Payne and his son making sausage. They jacked the car up and attached a grinder to the rear wheel, started up the motor, and voila, they had sausage!

In 1991, Mr. Payne sold the car to a broker, who sold it to Dennis Polk Equipment in Milford, Indiana. It was then sold to Don Hanson of Huntington, Indiana. My wife purchased the car from Don in 1995.

On a sunny day in June of 2001, Richard Payne called us from Andrews and said, "I wana see my car" (spoken with a country drawl). We gave him directions to our home, and he was there in ten minutes. When Mr. Payne saw "his car," he had tears running down his cheeks. He sat in the driver's seat but declined to take "his car" for a ride. That was the last we heard from Mr. Payne.

Richard Payne sitting in "his "car."

During the next couple of weeks, I asked around to find someone who knew about Model A's and was told about Todd Smith. Todd was an immense help with setting up who to call for parts and catalogues.

Life has many parts to it, not just cars. I had a dual knee replacement in March with a two-month recovery time, so not much happened with the car during that period. When I finally got healthy, I could not kneel. Restoring and fixing a Model A requires a lot of kneeling, so I needed to find a way to get to the floor. Throwing a rope over the garage rafter and holding on to it and lowering myself down to the floor worked well. It would be my plan from now on.

As the car was worked on, more issues surfaced. I settled on completing minor repairs such as tires, lights, wiring, and general maintenance. The car was painted in 2001 a 1996 Chrysler candy apple red color, which matched my wife's convertible of that description. We sometimes rode in parades with signs that read, his/hers or old/new. The speedometer was broken when we got the car. After talking with Richard Payne and Don Hanson, it was determined that the mileage of the car was 47,000.

In 1997, we joined the Old Fort Model A Club of Fort Wayne, Indiana. We jumped right into their activities and made many new friends. However, our first club tour was embarrassing. We ran out of gas! Now we carry an extra gallon of gas with us. It happens to most Model A'ers at some point in their excursions.

Abigail in body shop.

Abigail in paint shop.

A JOURNEY IN MILES AND BLESSINGS

Sharon writes:

As the years marched forward, we traveled to many places with the Old Fort Model A Club. Some of the more memorable trips include club trips as well as Model A Ford Club of America (MAFCA) and Model "A" Restorers Club (MARC) national tours to Texas, Alabama, Kentucky, Maine, and New York. On some of these excursions, we diverted from our fellow tour mates and took our own path home. Sometimes it was to go to states that were close by that we had not yet taken Abigail to. On the Maine trip, we headed for Connecticut and New Hampshire to visit with Bob Fisher, Tom's friend from his army days. The two had not seen each other since the end of their service deployment. On a national trip to Alabama, we took a long way home and added Georgia and Florida to our record. On another trip, Tom took our grandson Jaron and son Brian on the Pony Express and the Blue Ridge Parkway tours. Trips by ourselves included Pike's Peak, where Tom needed oxygen at the top (but Abigail was fine), and Yellowstone National Park with our collie, Spencer. After all these big trips, along with making every day journeys to the store, church, shopping, and local rides, we had accumulated 240,000 miles. Gradually, we had dipped our wheels in all but eight of the lower forty-eight states, including the District of

Columbia. That was our next challenge: get those last eight states.

This goal was not a huge bucket list burning desire but just a logical next step to take. In 2018 we were prodded forward by a $550 Christmas gift from our son and grandsons for seed money for the trip. After those gifts, it seemed like we had to do it now! So, we planned the trip and plotted out the route during the winter months.

When our actual departure day came, July 19, 2019, we had heavy hearts from the sudden death of our daughter. She died May 24, 2019, from a brief acute illness, four days after her forty-sixth birthday. During the months after her death, we were just surviving and running on automatic, trying not to feel too much. We were just putting one foot in front of the other and moving forward. So that is how we started the trip, low key, not too pumped up. Our mindset was "just get 'er done." We didn't plan to stop to sightsee; just "get 'er done."

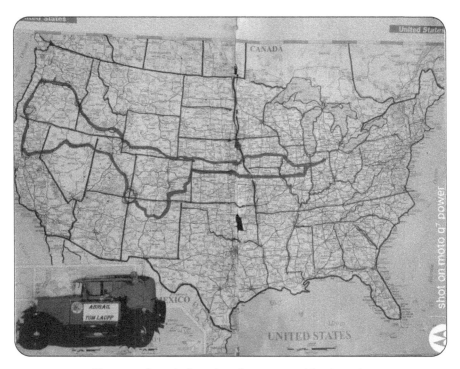

The route from Indiana heading west and back again.

DEPARTURE DAY

Friday, July 19

$\mathcal{L}$ ike most people who leave on vacation, we cleaned the house and had things buttoned up outside. Our pets were taken to their "vacation parents" the night before. They like staying with Barb and Terry, but we would miss them from the first day.

The departure morning was steamy and muggy. The temperature was already at 78 degrees. There was an extensive heat warning for that day and the next. That would be fun without air conditioning!

Three hours into our trip, we were in Illinois on US 24 with a temperature of 90 degrees. We met two bikers—high wheelers—traveling from Michigan to Missouri. Here is what they taught us. While we had our back seat full of stuff, each of them only carried a thin pack about twelve inches square strapped to their backs. That's it! And we made our first mistake of the trip; we did not get their names or a picture.

As we traveled west through Illinois, we reminisced about our nineteen years living there, 1969 to 1988. Tom travelled throughout the state as a territory manager for a floor covering company. Our children had swim meets in many of the towns on our route, and I toured on my bicycle through many of the same towns. That was in my younger years!

At mile 203, the temperature started to get hotter. We rode alongside the Illinois River at Peoria. Memories continued to flood us as we came to Eureka, Illinois, and Eureka College, where President Ronald Reagan attended school. It was also the site of an annual 230-mile bike ride I rode for ten consecutive years called PACRACC (or Pantagraph Area Cyclists Ride Around Corn Country). *The Pantagraph* was the local newspaper for Bloomington-Normal, Illinois, where we lived for nineteen years.

Our next memory jolt came as we rode through Canton, Illinois. This was the hometown of the very first owner of Abigail, John Adams. The next city we went through was Monmouth, Illinois, with the campus of Western Illinois University. Our son, Brian, attended his first year of college there. In 1989, he transferred to Purdue University in Lafayette, Indiana, the year after we moved to Indiana.

It was 3:00 pm, and we had travelled 326 miles. It was time to stop for our first overnight.

We were now in Moline, Illinois, and extremely hot in the un-airconditioned car. The temperature had been over 90 degrees for the last one and a half hours. We were ready for an air-conditioned room. Supper was at KFC, where we met Kathy and Mike Woodward. They told us about the area's finest ice cream shop, White's Ice Cream, and we had dessert with them there. This time, we were sure to get a picture!

DAY TWO

Saturday, July 20

*O*n day two, we left Moline at 6:49 am, Central time. Our bodies were still on Eastern time, so it was not too hard to get up early and get a head start on the day. That was important because there was an excessive heat warning that day. We did not have personal connections to the towns we travelled through that day as we had in Illinois.

We passed the famous Iowa 80 Truck Stop at 8:16 am. Tom and I had been there previously, so we did not stop.

Herbert Hoover is a "star" in Iowa. His presidential museum is located there.

This was the day we saw hundreds of bicyclists heading west for the start of the Register's Annual Great Bicycle Ride Across Iowa (RAGBRAI) in Council Bluffs, Iowa. RAGBRAI is a well-known 500-mile bike ride across Iowa from west to east, ending with the riders dipping their wheels in the Mississippi River. As these riders headed west to their starting point with their bikes in overhead carriers as well as other types of bike carriers, we passed and were passed by them repeatedly.

At one point, we stopped at a gas station at the same time as a group from Galena, a northern Illinois town. They were pumped up for their ride, and it was fun to talk to them. (Yes, we got a photo of them!) We could not stay too long; we had "promises to keep, And miles to go before we sleep."[1]

RAGBRAI riders

The expansive cornfields of Iowa looked like a huge, rippling velvet blanket. We had to make frequent stops for gasoline as our tank could only hold eleven gallons. This gave us the opportunity for potty breaks too. So, by 8:50 am, we were ready for both.

---

[1] Wikipedia. Robert Frost 1922 And quoted by John F Kennedy

Marshalltown came into view next. Our neighbors in Illinois, Jon and Judy Ward, were from there. The hills were getting longer and steeper now. There were extensive plantings of wildflowers along the banks of the highway, especially purple cone flowers and yellow daisies. We received a Facebook posting from our nephew Peter in Wisconsin that they were under a tornado warning. Some clouds were developing overhead for us too, and it was getting hotter.

We overnighted in Lincoln, Nebraska, at the Fairfield.

DAY THREE

Sunday, July 21

$\mathcal{S}$ unday morning started out to be very frustrating. Yes, car trouble! We tried to jump start the engine while still in the motel parking lot. We were all packed up and loaded for the day's trip. We had two major bouts of car problems on our trip. This was the first. It seemed to me that Tom enjoyed having these problems because it made the trip memorable for him. So, I will describe our turmoil!

All day, we could not get the car started. At 3:00 pm, we stopped for the day. Tom did lots of troubleshooting, including calling our friends Joe Baxter and Wayne Hull back in Indiana, the two experts in our Model A Club. They recommended changing the coil. Tom did that, and it made no difference, so that was not the problem.

Throughout our trip, we had just the right people come into our lives to assist us. A motel patron, Valerie, who was a FEMA (Federal Emergency Management Agency) worker here for a four-month assignment to assist Nebraska residents in their recovery from the spring floods, took us to Auto Zone two times.

That morning, we had thunderstorms with two and a half inches of rain. Since we had no transportation to get supper, we used Door Dash for the first time. Guess that makes us hip!

DAY FOUR

Monday, July 22

*M*onday morning at 7:30 am, Abigail would still not start, even using jumper cables. Tom made several calls to people on the National Model A roster. Thank goodness Curtis Griess answered our call and said he would be there in an hour. A motel patron Tom Czya was a super sleuth by discovering what looked like pure water in the sediment bowl instead of the expected gasoline. And yes, it was water in the gasoline tank! Problem solved. Praise the Lord!

So, the guys cleaned the carburetor and drained the visible water from the gas tank. Curtis got behind the wheel and started her up. After a short test drive, we were on the road again. Guess water in the gas tank is a better problem than some major mechanical breakdown! We were just meant to meet Valerie, Curtis, and Tom. Again, we felt so blessed and cared for. It was already 1:30 pm, so we stopped for lunch and gas. We hoped it was 100 percent gasoline this time!

Curtis Griess thinking of a plan to fix Abigail.

Tom Czya, the super sleuth detective.

We also took time to talk to several friends back home on the phone. We never lost touch with our friends and family during the trip.

We drove around Kearney, Nebraska, the sandhill crane capital of the world. The car was running well. The battery had full charge, the water temperature was 160-165 degrees, and the average speed was 50 mph. The posted speed on I-80 was 75 mph. Just past Buffalo Bill's ranch in North Platte, Nebraska, we called it a day. The total mileage for that day was 236 miles, but remember, we had a late start. The total trip was 944 miles to this point. Our grandson, Jaron, called. He was so lonely and missed his mom terribly. It was hard on us too. Jaron was just twenty-three years old when his mom, our daughter, died that past May. He was the one, with the help of our son Brian, who arranged his mom's funeral. It was all so sad. Tom and I were numb and just putting one foot in front of the other to move forward. It was hard to believe that our daughter was gone.

DAY FIVE

Tuesday, July 23

We pulled out of the Comfort Inn's parking lot at 7:35 am. Outside the temperature was 63 degrees. The sky was partially dark as we started Abigail up. We needed our jackets and traveled with the windows closed. Passing the Chimney Rock area, there were large, rectangular ponds alongside the highway.

At 7:57 am, the time zone changed to Mountain time, so it was now 6:57 am. That gave us a bonus hour. There were more hills and herds of cattle. At mile marker 145, there was a turnoff for the Fur and Trade Museum at Fort Atchison. That made us think of pioneer times and was a reminder that we were already in the wild, wild West. The trip mileage hit 1,000.2. There were huge feed lots of cattle. The elevation increased to 4,018 feet.

We took a bathroom break at Love's Truck Stop, which was at an elevation of 4,251 and was cold and windy. Now the speed limit on I-80 was 80 mph. There were sunflowers planted alongside the highway and oil or natural gas wells in the fields. Just like back home, road construction was everywhere, even at an elevation of 5,056 feet.

At 10:54 am, we crossed into Wyoming. We had 399 miles to get to its western border. With all the states we had traveled in so far on this trip, we had already driven Abigail in them on previous trips. Getting to the eight states we needed to complete our goal was taking a long time. There were many gates to close the road in case of dangerous weather. A fancy wrought iron sign on ranchland with cattle said, "It's What's for Supper." We were climbing higher and higher. At Cheyenne, Wyoming, our lunch stop, the elevation was 6,408. Our afternoon brought elevations to 8,640 feet (about the length of 30 city blocks). Points of interest included Medicine Bow National Forrest; huge, tall, multiple snow fences; Abraham Lincoln's statue on a hillside; very steep, 5 percent downgrade roads; University of Wyoming at Larami; Butch Cassidy Museum; Sand Creek Massacre Trail; and Outlaws Inn & Frontier Prison at Rawlings. We overnighted in the Comfort Inn. We did not record our mileage for the day.

DAY SIX

Wednesday, July 24

*I*t was 6:50 am as we left Rawlings, Wyoming, hoping to make it to Utah that day. It was 105 miles to Rock Springs. That was where Abigail had broken down on our Yellowstone trip in 2012. At 7:11 am, we were at an elevation of 7,000 feet. We passed the Continental Divide, only to re-pass it two more times on the trip. The terrain was bleak and desert-like. Oil wells were pumping throughout the countryside. A sign indicated a "Strong Wind Area."

At 7:49 am, the friend we had met the day before at the motel gave a "toot" as he passed us in his older Chevy truck. He was bound for Oregon, about 600 miles ahead. He traveled twice a year to Florida to visit his mother.

At 8:36 am, a bathroom break was needed. The facility was a partial passive solar building. This was across the highway from where Abigail had limped to a stop with her broken crankshaft in 2012 on that famous Yellowstone trip. It was very cold and breezy. We passed Exit 139 to Red Hill Road and a big quarry. The elevation was 6,879. Then we descended.

The area was very desolate and tough driving due to steep climbs and descents. There were parking areas after the long climbs. Just like back home, we experienced road construction. It was 8:49 am when we spotted the first train traveling east today. Tom *loves* trains! At least we never had to come to a complete stop.

At 9:10 am, the first windmill blade we had seen in five days was being transported east. The next high-lights on our trip that day included Rock Springs, Green River, Flamingo Gorge, and Little America, where its sign said, "Relax, Your Shower is Waiting" with seventeen marble showers.

At 10:14 am, we were at an elevation of 6,402 feet, back in the desert, and on the way to Salt Lake City, Utah. There was an American flag on the top of a hill, cattle at an elevation of 7,279 feet, and a wind farm on the crest of a long hill. Tom had to shift going downhill. At 12:30 pm, we made it to Utah. One state down, seven more to go!

Utah is named after the Native American tribe Ute, which means "people of the mountains."[2]

The Great Salt Lake is the largest lake west of the Mississippi River. The mountains near Salt Lake City average 500 inches of snowfall per year. Utah's admission to statehood was January 4, 1896, (the nation's forty-fifth state). Utah is in Mountain time and is comprised of mountains, high plateaus, and deserts forming most of its landscape. Its population is 3 million, qualifying as the thirtieth most populous state and the thirteenth largest

---

[2] Google. Uta Native American Tribe.

by area. Popular destinations are Zion National Park, Bryce Canyon National Park, and Arches National Park. [3]

The Great Salt Lake

A little more than half of all Utahns are Mormons, the vast majority of whom are members of the Church of Jesus Christ of Latter-day Saints (LDS Church), which has its world headquarters in Salt Lake City. Utah is the only state in which most of the population belongs to a single church.[4]

---

[3] Google. State of Utah

[4] Google. Mormon Church and Utah

We moved from Interstate 80 to I-84. There was snow on the mountain tops, rock climbers in the distance and rafters on a river nearby. We passed a train—wow, something slower than us! We overnighted in Logan, Utah.

DAY SEVEN

Thursday, July 25

*I*t was 6:50 am. We were leaving Logan, Utah, after backtracking there the day before because there had been no affordable motels where we initially stopped. So, I had to try to stop thinking of the back-tracking hour and just focus on moving forward. But we could have been two hours further west by now if we had not backtracked! We were traveling west on I-84 toward Idaho. The terrain was mountainous, and even a climb of a couple hundred feet was steep. The miles in the mountains are slower, so it takes longer to make progress.

At 8:01 am, a sign indicated that Idaho was only fifteen miles ahead. There were only ranch exits off the highway, no services. The wheat fields were huge. Rattlesnake Pass was at Exit 17 with an elevation of 5,302 feet. We were getting closer to getting to the second state of our quest. Now it was only four miles to Snowville, the border of Idaho.

At 8:22 am, we made it to Idaho. It was exhilarating to know we were certainly now on the path to our goal. It was happening! That called for a break, so bathroom for us and gas for Abigail.

State signs on opposite sides of the road.

Idaho is known for its mountainous landscapes and vast swaths of protected wilderness and outdoor recreation areas. The capitol, Boise, is set in the Rocky Mountains foothills. Idaho's known for its potatoes, but it's official nickname is the Gem State. Some seventy-two different precious and semi-precious gemstones have been found there. Points of interest include Craters of the Moon, Shoshone Falls Park, and the Oregon Trail. Idaho became the forty-third state on July 3, 1890 and is the fourteenth largest state. The 2019 population of Idaho was 1.787 million, making it the twelfth least populated state.[5]

We had a long way to go, so the stop was quick. Posted on the highway was a sign saying, "Fire Danger is High Today" and another sign that said, "Deer Migration Path for 10 miles." Switzer Summit was located at 5,500 feet.

The next turnoff was for City of Rocks. A van passed by us with a sign that read, "Rocky Mt. Rodeo Team." The air was now very hazy, and soon, a sign popped up warning, "Dust Storm Areas-No Stopping on Highway." The terrain was flat now but would not stay that way for long. We would take the flat miles as long as they lasted!

At Exit 216 was Pomerville Ski Area. At 10:47 am, we found a motel converted into a Travelodge and Phillip's 66 gas station. A yellow crop duster was spraying fields. The ranchers here were serious about their hay storage. Huge bales of hay were neatly covered with blue and white tarps. A business sign advertised "Laser Land Leveling."

---

[5] Google. State of Idaho

At 1:17 pm, we saw the first of three huge feed lots. Our travels took us northwest toward Oregon and Washington. Semi-trucks can have three trailers in this area. The mountains were getting much closer—ugh. There was evidence of large fires along the roadside. At mile marker 148 and an elevation of 3,209 feet, there were wind farms. We were listening to "Davy Crocket-King of the Wild Frontier" on our tapes—seemed appropriate. The speed limit was 80 mph. We were at an elevation of 2,798, and we could see in the distance that we would be going back up.

The Snake River with wind farms in the distance.

Passing Glenn's Ferry and the Snake River, we were indeed in the mountains again. A road sign said, "Frequent High

Winds." Tom said, "Steady—not frequent," as he struggled to keep the car on a straight path.

At 12:25 pm, we stopped for lunch and gas at Mountain Home City. Making it to Oregon was our goal that day. It was a hot drive, with the temperature in the nineties. I gave Tom one of the iced neck wraps that we kept in the cooler. We also had a plan to drink more water. There was a police car on our side of the road. They did not chase us since we did not have enough horses in the engine to speed!

We drove around Boise, Idaho, with seventeen miles to Ontario, Oregon, where we quit for the day. Our total trip miles to date were 2,032. Now we had reached the third state of eight.

Oregon is known as the "Beaver State." It was admitted to the Union as the thirty-third state on February 14,1859 and is the fourteenth largest state and the twenty seventh most populous[6]. The Columbia River delineates much of Oregon's northern boundary with Washington while the Snake River delineates much of its eastern boundary with Idaho.

Oregon comprises an area of startling physical diversity, from the moist rain forest, mountains, and fertile valleys of its western third to the naturally arid and climatically harsh eastern desert. Forests cover more than two-fifths

---

[6] Google, State of Oregon

of Oregon. Nationally, Oregon ranks at or near the top among all states in the production of wood products.[7]

One of the state's principal tourist destinations is Mount Hood National Forest. Other attractions include Crater Lake, a spectacular blue lake with a huge volcanic caldera, and Mount Hood, the highest peak in Oregon at 11,239 feet.

Almost one-fourth of all Oregonians live in three cities, Portland, Eugene, and Salem. Portland is a leading west coast port.[8] We were headed to the Rogue River Valley, whose major cities are Grants Pass, Ashland, and Medford.

---

[7] Google. State of Oregon

[8] Google . Oregon

DAY EIGHT

Friday, July 26

$\mathcal{S}$ tarting out from Ontario, Oregon, on I-84, I did not get the picture of the "Weedology" store that I wanted to take. Bummer. We had passed the store the previous night coming into Ontario, but leaving that morning, we could not find it.

The temperature was 66, and there were clear skies. At 7:02 am, we were at an elevation of 2,151 feet. A sign indicated we were in a "Snow Zone." Also, there was a sign for Huntington, at twenty-six miles away. Did we take the wrong turn? (We live eight miles from Huntington, Indiana!)

Suddenly, some dark clouds appeared overhead, and it began to sprinkle a little. Desert-like rugged hills loomed in the distance. Oh my gosh, there were mountains after mountains. There were also guardrails along the road. You could see directly over the edge—no room for highway side ditches or sunflowers.

At 7:30 am, it became 6:30 am as we passed into the Pacific time zone. Wow, we had not left yet!

We travelled past the following areas without problems: Van Ornum Battleground, Burnt River, Rye Valley, the

Last Dutchman mining camp, and a train tunnel. At Exit 330, a huge cement plant caught our attention. Although these cites sounded interesting, we did not stop to investigate; we kept moving forward. By 8:58 am, we had put 148 miles behind us, mostly due to our gift of an additional hour when we'd changed time zones. Exit 228 was Deadman's Pass and the first warning of an upcoming 6 percent downgrade ahead. It had a breakout area. Exit 216 sported a casino. A red convertible with its top down passed us. We used to have one of them and loved to ride with the top down. Large solar fields were a common sight in this area.

Another climb. Another sign promised "Blowing Desert Area Next 40 Miles." Stage Gulch boasted having the Pendleton airport. We passed a "fantastically" (Tom's word) large wheat field. Sunflowers grew along the roadside. Nine motorcyclists dressed in Harley garb passed us. Workers were hand-picking low-growing crops in a field. They had a port-a-potty on the back of a pickup truck parked in the field.

At 8:40 am, we came to Exit 186. Stansfield-Hermiston was our gas and restroom stop. Washington State was ninety-two miles ahead. We were heading to the north border of Oregon and had just passed Umatilla Army Depot, Arlington, Boardman with a water park and sprinklers and the Umatilla Indian reservation. At Exit 147, Ione and Hoepper are cities near the site of a large reservoir lake over a mile long. Three-mile Canyon is to the left.

At 12:16 pm, we had lunch at The Bulldog. The server told us about the next exit on the right would be a bridge into the state of Washington. So, our plan was to cross the bridge into Washington, take a picture, return across the bridge into Oregon, and continue our trip. So, Washington was the state we spent the least time in. But yippie! We now had four states under our belt. Halfway done! Having dipped our wheels into Washington, that completed our northernmost point of the trip. So, in a way, that was a turning point to the way home.

Abigail and Sharon at Washington State marker.

Washington State is the thirteenth most populous and eighth largest state and is called "The Evergreen State." Statehood was granted on November 11, 1889. Washington is the only state named after a president.

Washington produces the most apples of all the states. Over 1,000 dams dot its landscape. Medina is the home of one of the United States wealthiest men, Microsoft's Bill Gates. Major attractions are Seattle and the Space Needle, Olympic National Park, Mount Rainier and Mount Rainier National Park, and the Hoh Rainforest.[9]

As we followed I-84 West along the northern border of Oregon to Portland, we passed the City of The Dalles, the largest city on the Oregon side along the Columbia River outside of Portland. The traffic approaching Portland was horrendous. There was an auto accident, so lanes were closed, and traffic was stopped at times. It was 4:16 pm, and I-5 was backed up in four lanes for miles. We were creeping along.

A scene approaching Portland, Oregon.

---

[9] Google . State of Washington

We got gas in Lake Oswego and began looking for a hotel room. We were so ready to get out of the car, so we decided to take a motel we found regardless of price. It was in a fancy location, so our fingers were crossed that it would be okay. However, I didn't unbuckle my seat belt until I knew for sure whether we would be staying there!

There were a lot of soccer tournament kids and their parents checking in to the motel as well, kids of all ages dressed for soccer. Today would have been too hot for us to have taken our two dogs along. Then, yay—it was settled that we were staying the night at this Comfort Inn!

As you read this saga, you might wonder, "How did she remember all the little towns and elevations?" I decided to take notes to be sure I did not fall asleep. Riding in the passenger seat is a spot prone to dozing. I thought, *Tom is doing all the driving. He cannot take a nap. So, I will not either.*

Amazingly, I was not sleepy during the entire trip. I would take notes during the daily excursions. Then, in the evening, I would rewrite the narrative in better penmanship. The original notes were not easy to decipher. Writing legibly in a bouncy car is difficult. I typed this story from the rewritten notes.

DAYS NINE AND TEN

Saturday, July 27, and Sunday, July 28

*W*e were en route to my longtime friend Joan Vaughter's home in Wilderville, Oregon, 248 miles away. We traveled on I-5 South. That may not sound like many miles, but remember, these were mountain miles. We passed Wilsonville, Darala, and Mt. Angel before traveling through Salem, the state capitol. Still traveling south on I-5, we passed turnoffs for Albany, Lebanon, and Corvallis.

My great Aunt Chic moved to Corvallis from West Allis, Wisconsin. She lived to be 101 years old. Our family visited her when I was a child. That was my first long road trip. At mile marker 247, you can find the "Grass Seed Capital of the World." We passed large tree nurseries. They must have used gallons of Roundup because there were no weeds at all. We could see more mountains in the distance. Oh, I hoped we could miss them. (What did I think, a trip to the West Coast would be devoid of mountains? No, I knew it wouldn't be, but they are scary to drive through with drop-offs and curves and steep climbs and descents.) But we were going to make it through!

At 8:55 am, we had traveled seventy-five miles. We now had mountains on both sides of us, but we were going through the middle of them. There were 208 miles to

California, but that was not our immediate goal today. We just needed to get to Wilderville, which is south of Grants Pass.

The Mohawk and McKenzie Rivers are at Eugene, Oregon, home of the University of Oregon and the Oregon "Ducks". Next on our route was Klamath Falls and the Applegate Trail. A blue and bright yellow log truck caught our eye. It was for sale.

At 11:25 am, we observed a wildfire, which was burning over 9,000 acres (about half the area of Cleveland, Ohio) and was not under control yet. You could smell the smoke in the air. That was somewhat alarming.

Oregon forest fires.

Abigail making her way through the smoke.

Oakland, Sutherlin, Canyonville, Wolf Creek, and Crater Lake were next on our route to pass through or by. There were many snow zones marked along the highway. The smoke got heavier at times, and we saw exactly where the fires were burning. At Exit 71, driving around Sunny Valley, we passed a tanker with a double trailer. He must not have minded an eighty-nine-year-old-car passing him because he waved and tooted his horn. The elevation was 1,913 feet.

Oh, no, I looked out the window and over the side rails. That was my least favorite thing to do! The last 210 miles had been mountain miles, all with smoke from the forest fires. Tom was having a little trouble breathing because he has COPD (from his parents smoking). He took a puff from his inhaler and felt a little better. At Hugo, Exit 66, we had only ten miles to get to Grants Pass. It was still hilly and smoky. At 12:19 pm and Exit 61, we drove through Merlin and over the Rouge River. Grants Pass was at Exit 58, where we stopped and had lunch.

Upon entering Grants Pass, we were off I-5. There were just eight more miles to Joan's at Wilderville. We got there but not before calling Joan three times for clarification of the directions. Somehow the area did not look anything like I remembered from our trip in 1999. Finally, we got turned around and found Joan's home, Flowing River Farm. Staying here for two days would give us the opportunity to catch up on old times.

Joan and I met in first grade at Mother of Good Counsel School in Milwaukee, Wisconsin. We stayed connected throughout high school at Divine Savior Prep School and then Marquette University, all in Milwaukee. Then we went our separate ways but never lost touch. I am so blessed to have Joan as one of my best friends. Growing up, our families were close too. Joan's dad was my dentist.

Joan and her guard dog Max sitting in the golf cart.

When we girls were young, we had planned to have a pig farm together. Joan is a huge animal lover and had a vast variety of animals in her childhood. I only had cats, dogs, turtles, and fish. Today on Joan's twenty-acre farm, you will see chickens, goats, donkeys, one cow, two horses, cats, three dogs—Max and Marlie, both Great Pyrenees crosses, and Baxter, her retired therapy dog—rabbits, and birds in an aviary. Irrigation for the farm is supplied through a ditch every ten days for a seven-hour flow. Sometimes one's turn to get water may come in the middle of the night for a fee of $600 per month. Because forest fires are such a frequent threat in Oregon, people stay prepared to cope with the adverse effects of them. At the back door of Joan's home, there is a hook for masks to be worn when going outside. Joan's daughter, Kari, lives in her own brand-new home on the property with her boyfriend, Mark, as well as Joan's grandson, Grayson, who lives in his own two-story chalet close to the Applegate River. Kari, Grayson, and Mark are a huge support for Joan. They help with many of the farm chores and certainly give Joan a sense of security and family. They do things together but still have the space to do their own things. We met Joan's next-door neighbor, Kathy Lay, and toured her lovely home. We were in awe of her prize-winning gladioluses.

Tom and Mark wearing smoke protection masks
while taking a walk on the farm.

Of course, our time at Joan's went by quickly. We had a delicious taco supper at Kari's the night we arrived and supper the night before we left at River's Edge Restaurant. We sat outside on the terrace with the Rouge River flowing just feet away. It was, indeed, a beautiful and peaceful setting. It was a wonderful reunion, and I left promising Joan that I would return in 2020 to celebrate her eightieth birthday and take the traditional swim in the Applegate River with her and her friends.

As I write this account of our trip, little did any of us realize the entire world would be hit with the COVID-19 pandemic in the spring of 2020. Because of the pandemic, I will not be traveling to Oregon to "dip in the river" and celebrate Joan's milestone birthday.

DAY ELEVEN

Monday, July 29

*W*e left Joan's at 7:04 am. We had said goodbye to Kari, Mark, Grayson, the three dogs, and the barn animals the night before. Now just one last hug to Joan, and we were off. On the way out, we passed the balloons Joan placed on her gate to welcome us. They read, "You made it!" Yes, we certainly did!

At 7:38 am, we met up with I-5 again at Grants Pass and headed for California. The elevation was 1,893 feet at the "Snow Zone" area. We passed Medford. After Ashland and the Klamath Falls turn off, we were at a greater elevation of 2,238 and again in a "Snow Zone/Chains Required" section of the highway. Mt. Ashland is at an elevation of 7,535 feet (about twice the height of the Burj Khalifa, the tallest building in the world) and eight miles away from California. Abigail had huge hills to climb and then go back down, many with a 6 percent grade.

At 8:40 am, we entered California. Only three more states to go! To many people, including me, California seems like a utopia. California is the most populous state and has 40 million residents (about twice the population of New York). Nicknamed the "Golden State," it is the third largest state and was admitted to the Union on September 9, 1850.

California is insanely diverse with sun-kissed surf beaches, fascinating cities, picturesque vineyards, rugged mountains, soaring redwood forests, and dramatic deserts. With millions of acres of farmland, California leads the United States in agriculture production. Hilly San Francisco is known for the Golden Gate Bridge, Alcatraz island, and cable cars. The city of Los Angeles is the seat of the Hollywood entertainment industry. One should not forget Disneyland, Yosemite National Park, and Angel Island.[10]

As soon as we were in California, we found ourselves on a road going down from an elevation of 2,789 feet with a 4 percent grade and a sign saying, "Brakeless Trucks Use Left Lane." The next sign read, "Stop Ahead All Cars – No Fruit or Plants Allowed." The morning temperature was a comfortable 72 degrees.

---

[10] Google. California

We came off the highway into the town of Yreka to use the restroom and get gas. I gave a homeless man sitting on the curb two bags of candy that Joan had given us for the trip. I wish I had had some dog treats for his black and white dog. As we left the gas station, there was a deer with two fawns running along the fence on our right side. I hoped they would not get hit by a car or truck. Mt. Shasta was off to our left with an elevation of 14,162 feet (about half the cruising altitude of a commercial jet).

Since we'd left the Medford, Oregon, area, we had been travelling through multiple national forests, mountains, and wilderness areas. When going through the Trinity National Forest, it started to get smoky again, enough that Tom had to use his inhaler.

Driving south past Exit 391, we passed Bead Butte Summit and the Sacramento River and could still see the snowcapped tips of Mt. Shasta on our left. There was a bear crossing sign that pictured a momma and baby bear. Traveling these California mountains, we were on the inside lane going down, which I preferred over the treacherous other side of the road. By 10:30 am, the temperature had risen to 89 degrees. At Exit 712, we went by Pollard Pass and could see evidence of pre-vious forest fires. Whiskeytown is at Exit 685, as well as the city of Shasta Lake. The elevation was only 767 feet. Redding, at Exit 682, was our lunch, gas, and Wi-Fi stop. Then we headed back into the mountains, where it was getting ridiculously hot. We heard that it was raining back home in Indiana. At this point, both of us were using the cooling neck wraps.

Pink flowers were cascading over the hills along with white flowering bushes. Many orchards dotted the countryside, some with olive trees and others with almond. Again, there were no weeds or grass in the rows. At Exit 633, Richfield, the ditches were all dried up. We lost the mountains at Redding. The temperature was now 95 degrees, and traffic had increased.

At 2:04 pm, we were now on Highway 230 heading east. The mountains were in the distance. We had planned to overnight in Yuba City, but no rooms were available. So, it was on to Marysville and the Comfort Inn. We had changed our route plans that day to Highway 20 to avoid travelling through Sacramento, where we had originally planned to catch I-80. Our total miles of the day topped off at 315, with total trip miles measured at 3,080.6 miles (about the width of the United States). We had supper at Tracy's, a restaurant with a real car cut apart and made into seating areas.

DAY TWELVE

Tuesday, July 30

*L*eaving Marysville, California, at 6:30 am found us experiencing fair weather with a temperature of 61 degrees. The expected high for the day was 93 degrees. Our first day of heading east kept the sun shining in our eyes for hours. Tom commented, "Driver screw-up," because the passenger windshield was streaky. It could be fixed at the next gas stop.

Road construction stopped traffic completely on Highway 20, which was a contrast to construction on interstates, which only closes one lane, allowing traffic to proceed. The interstates are easier for us to travel, but since we had chosen this way in order to bypass Sacramento, our path was going to be more difficult. The grade of climb and descent was greater, and there were more curves and sharp drop-offs along the edge of the road. I kept telling myself, "I've been to the top of Pikes Peak in this car, so this should be a piece of cake." Nevertheless, I would be happy when we were off this road.

Ascending to 3,870 feet from 1,300 feet, Abigail was in regular third gear then high second gear to low third to high second. The Tahoe National Forest surrounded us.

At 7:55 am, the temperature remained comfortable at 72 degrees. The climb continued to 5,335 feet (about half the height of Mount St. Helens). We pulled over and let twelve cars and one truck pass us. It was easier for me to tolerate these high altitudes in the forest than be on the outside edge of a mountain. Two miles of a steep grade descent followed our climb. The engine did some of the braking. Tom used fourth gear then high third on the descent to 4,000 feet (about half the length of the Golden Gate Bridge) then back up to 5,230.

That was quite a challenging morning so far. I-80 heading toward Reno, Nevada, should make travel a little easier. At 8:28 am, we were in "Snow and Chain Installation Areas" at 6,000 feet. The temperature dropped to 65 degrees at Kingsvale, where we took a bathroom and gas break and purchased a Lake Tahoe, California, T-shirt and postcards. At Soda Springs, the Donner's Pass road boasts elevations of 7,125 feet and a steep downhill. Tom shifted into regular third using engine instead of brake pedal then overdrive. Mountains in this area belong to the Sierra Mountain range.

Traveling north of Lake Tahoe on the California side, the roads continued to be mountainous. Heading east to Nevada was a downhill ride on I-80 with 5 percent grade. The clock marked our passage into Nevada at 9:30 am. Two more states to go, Arizona and New Mexico.

We reached Nevada, the sixth state in our quest.

Nevada was made famous by the 1859 discovery of the Comstock Lode, the richest known U.S. silver deposit. Nevada is the largest gold-producing state in the nation and is second in the world behind South Africa. Nevada is also the gambling and entertainment capital of the United States.[11]

We encountered a slight delay in our forward progress as we stopped in Reno for an oil change, grease job, and wheel balance and rotation. Standing still from 9:55 am to 12:20 pm, I had had no idea that Tom was planning that stop. Oh, well, I guess the car needed it. A round-about in the shopping center where we had the work done was a first for us. We had traveled 121 miles for

---

[11] Google . Nevada

the day, and the total trip miles were 3,210. Tom said, "The wheels feel much better."

The next twenty minutes after we started back up put us right back into the mountains. Upcoming locations included Lockwood, Mustang, USA Parkway-Highway 439, Painted Rock, Wadsworth, Pyramid Lake, Great Basin National Park, and the Nevada Pacific Parkway. The wind was very gusty and bounced Abigail around. The temperature was 95 degrees. It was twenty-two miles to Lovelock, where we would gas up and have that necessary potty stop. Our plan was to overnight in Winnemucca, ninety-four miles ahead.

Lovelock is situated in the desert. The gas station should have been labeled as a liquor store. All the shelves were stocked with liquor bottles of all sizes and shapes. Michelle, the store clerk, laughed as we reacted to the scene. She gave us permission to take her picture. The restroom had a portable, plug-in hand dryer. A twelve-foot slice of a redwood tree was displayed in the parking lot. The countryside was sprinkled with rundown houses.

Gas station or liquor store?

At 2:30 pm, we were riding at an elevation of 4,006 feet (about the length of fifteen city blocks) by cattle grazing in a pasture. Signs for "Chain and Snow Tires Required" and a correctional center with a "No Hitchhiking" sign were posted along the route. Exit 112 announced Coal Canyon, Oreana, and Rochester. Our elevation climbed to 4,220 feet. A train with no engine was parked on the tracks alongside the road. Tom could go there at night and paint graffiti on the cars! Rye Patch Dam was at Exit 129. A family walking on the highway with a car parked on the side of the road waved us on as no need to help. The town of Humbolt at Exit 136 warned that no services were available. At 4,329 feet and an outside temperature of 95 degrees, we were sweating, even in our elbows. The cooling neckbands and lots of water helped us through those hot miles.

Still climbing to 4,436 feet (about the elevation of Denver, Colorado), Abigail was doing great. I guess she liked her treat of an oil change and grease job! Cattle were grazing in a monstrous field. It seemed they must be hot with no protection from this baking sun. I sure hoped they had enough water. Injecting a little humor, Tom said, "This dry weather sure does dry out your boogers!"

A little consternation to top off our day—no rooms in Lovelock. Winnemucca would be our next stop. After the second motel, we found our room for the night. The shortage of rooms in this rural area was due to a livestock auction.

DAY THIRTEEN

Wednesday, July 31

At 6:30 am, an early start should help us get through Nevada and on to Salt Lake City. We were plodding our way to the "Four Corners" to complete our quest of all the lower forty-eight states. That goal could not come soon enough.

We looked for a McDonald's but could not find it. It was probably within some other store like we had seen the previous night with a Dairy Queen inside a grocery store. Today's ride saw us climbing to 5,150 feet to Golconda Summit and then right back down again.

Iron Point and Pumpernickel Valley were next on our route. More signs were posted that snow chains were required. Making forward progress at 7:22 am, Battle Mountain was in our sights. This town had a water tower, hospital, visitor center, and golf course.

Next in our path was the town of Emigrant, with a tough climb to 6,094 feet. Then—you know the routine—what goes up must come down. The descent was a steep decline, but Abigail's high gear was holding fine. Technically, we should have been in third gear because that was what we'd used climbing up. There were tall cement guardrails long the road. Yes! The highways were busy with many things. We spotted Army equipment being transported. At the Elko County line, we came through another prison area with "No Hitchhiking" signs posted. Coming down the mountain, at 4,922 feet, a tunnel saved us some stress of climbing and descending. The train had its own tunnel too. An interesting warning sign read, "When Shooting from the Road, There is a Penalty."

Elko was the last city on I-80 before we reached Utah, and it had an airport. Nevada certainly felt like "cowboy and Indian" territory. High peaks in this area include Pilot Peak, sitting at 10,716 feet, Pequop Summit at 7,005 feet, and Hole in the Mountain Peak at 11,306 feet.

As we traveled I-80 east through the Nevada Desert to the Utah border, we experienced the Great Salt Lake Desert. The Great Salt Lake Desert is a large dry lake in northern Utah between the Great Salt Lake and the Nevada border, which is noted for white evaporite Lake Bonneville salt deposits."[12] One's first glance at the Great Salt Lake Desert, and you'd think it is snow, but it is salt deposits.

Somewhere during our miles crossing the Great Salt Lake Desert, our car passed the 300,000-mile reading on our odometer. We noticed this milestone when we looked down at the odometer and it read 300,010 miles. That was the total actual recorded miles on Abigail, not what we personally achieved. Personally, we were at 250,000 miles. The additional miles were recorded by previous owners. The third owner of Abigail said the odometer

---

[12] Google .Great Salt Lake Desert

was not working when he bought the car. That leaves the possibility that Abigail might even have more miles than the recorded 300,000.

Just like at home, road construction is inevitable and occurs often, even in the desert and mountains. We began another tough climb to 6,000 feet. "Come on, little car, you can do it!" we told her. A rest area at 6,950 sported an outhouse; it was okay. We caught up to the "Living the Dream" RV that had passed us earlier. Several "Cattle Crossing" tunnels were in our path. This is where traffic uses the tunnel and cattle use a wide grass-covered causeway that runs over the road. .

At 6,238 feet, Abigail's temperature decreased to 140 from 190 degrees at the summit. Oh, no—a tragedy! Our M&M's were all gone! I believe many travelers must think like we did, just amazed at the pioneers who made the westward trip in covered wagons. How did they ever accomplish their feat? It is not easy even in a modern car. While on our journey, phone calls from our back-home friends were a treasure. Carolyn Minick called that day, and each day, our neighbor Barb Myers, our dogs' "vaca-tion mother," texted us to say the furry kids were good. We looked forward to her reassuring text each day.

Salt Lake City was ten miles ahead. The landscape was flat, and the speed limit was 80 mph, so, driving at that speed, one mile should take forty-five seconds. We did not have to worry about that, however, as there was a speedometer check on the road.

The outside temperature registered at 96 degrees, and the wind was strong. Tom was a trooper, keeping everything under control. Gee, I am glad I married him! Things were flying around in the car and needed to be re-secured. The cooling neck wraps came in handy again. The wind had our speed down to 45 mph, but we were still going forward. Suddenly, the outside temperature dropped 10 degrees. I wondered if it was raining somewhere.

We made an emergency stop so Tom could check the radiator because the engine was not cooling as it should. Tom found the fan belt very loose. With a little adjustment, we were rolling again. The outside temperature continued to drop, a mystery! A phone call came in at 1:55 pm with an invitation from Dee Kochensparger at the Andrews-Dallas Township Public Library in Andrews, Indiana, to give a talk on September 11th about this trip. We felt like such celebrities!

Traveling east, we lost time as the time changed from 2:28 pm Pacific time to 3:28 pm Mountain time. We decided to call it quits for the day as we made it to our destination, Salt Lake City. As we surmised about the temperature decreasing, it was raining extremely hard upon our arrival.

An overnight in the Micro Motel convinced us not to choose Micro gain. It was low-end budget style. One awesome feature at the Micro, however, was a huge welcome sign in the dining room in many languages. Salt Lake City is a "Sanctuary City."

Welcome sign in Micro Motel.

DAY FOURTEEN

Thursday, August 1

*L*eaving the Microtel Motel in Salt Lake City at 6:55 am, it was a sunny 66 degrees. There was a little mix up with the roads as it took us a couple of tries to get going in the right direction. Tom said, "We just took a tour!"

Salt Lake City is a large, busy city with five lanes of heavy traffic. That day, we were heading south on 215 to I-15 toward Las Vegas. We were going to cut off I-15 before it got to Las Vegas. We could almost taste our victory as we came closer to reaching the Four Corners. Would we get there today? Only time would tell. I missed a cool photo opportunity to shoot a red, white, and blue commuter train on its journey south because I did not have my camera ready.

The mountains had houses sprinkled along their ridges. Soon after Salt Lake City, we were traveling in those mountains again. These were scary roads with curves and drop offs. Of course, we had to have our daily dose of construction. Escorts were provided by a highway pickup truck through the diversion.

We had been climbing ever since leaving Salt Lake City. By 10:30 am, we were at 7,459 feet. Signs proclaimed,

"Sharp Curves Ahead" and "Chain Up Area Ahead." It was amazing how quickly the scene changed. By 10:35 am, a plateau gave us "an easy street." But by the next ten minutes, scary was back. A 7 percent downhill grade was our companion, along with gusty winds. At least the road was straight. We had accumulated 129 miles so far for the day.

It looked like it would be another day of low miles due to mountain (slow) miles. The next turn onto Route 6 at Spanish Fork took us off the main highway and onto a secondary road. There was another climb and then a 3 to 5 percent downhill grade. Today was not for the faint-hearted. Oh, my gosh, I did not even want to look out the window, but I still took a picture.

At 10:15 am, Ginny Thomas from the dog club we belong to returned my call. She was undergoing chemo-therapy treatments and said she had just experienced the worst surgery she had ever had. What can you say to a friend who is in this situation? Not much, just listen and offer your support. Ginny's dog is Finn, a huge, gentle Newfoundland.

So many miles separated us from home, but we were not disconnected. Route 6 was taking us southeast to 191 toward Four Corners. Would we make it there that day? Stay tuned.

Exiting the highway at Price led to a surprise, a town with trees, grass, and a real community. The streets near the gas station were dotted with colorful sculptures. It was a treat to see something besides desert and bareness. We passed I-70, which goes east and west, and the town of Green River.

Every mile in the mountains is well earned and not easy. We were making incredibly slow progress, and it was already 1:35 pm. Monticello, Utah, was thirty-two miles ahead. That might be as far as we get for the day. We were hoping to meet our goal, but there were strong headwinds. Always something! A super bug flew inside the car. I squashed him and threw him out and said to myself, "This is going to be a long day."

Monument Valley in southeastern Utah is home to some of the most iconic rock formations on earth. It features miles of open flat desert contrasted by giant sandstone buttes jutting hundreds of feet into the sky. This area has been used for the setting of many western films.[13]

Passing Hole 'N the Rock, a spectacular sight, people were hiking and exploring there. That would be cool to do, but Tom and my days for doing that are over.

The Hole '"N the Rock is forty miles north of Monticello and is a famous roadside landmark. Blasted out of solid rock by local resident Niele and Jean Christensen, the landmark includes a large home, petting zoo, and plenty of unexpected surprises.[14]

---

[13] Bayley Hedglin, "Welcome to San Juan Country," *Utah's Canyon* Country," 2019, 22.

[14] Bayley Hedglin, "Welcome to San Juan Country," *Utah's Canyon Country*, 2019. 32.

Monticello, at 7,520 feet, was our refuge for the night. It is called "The Land Above the Canyons." Today's mileage was 270 miles. Tomorrow, we should get to the Four Corners. The plan was to take a picture and post it on Facebook then head home!

Note: At 3:00 am on August 2nd, Tom woke up having trouble breathing. I did too, but mine felt like a panic attack. Tom took a dose from his rescue inhaler and obtained some relief. I wondered if I should have contacted the front desk and had him taken to a hospital, wherever one was.

It felt like we were in the middle of nowhere. Were we going to be able to complete our goal? It seemed doubtful now. I wondered if he would have to be flown out of this little town and if we would have to fly back to Indiana and have our car and belongings trucked back. It was a worrisome night, thinking, *Oh, we are so close to achieving our goal but just on the edge of not being able to "get it done."* We prayed for a good resolution, and somehow, both of us settled down and fell asleep for a few more hours.

DAY FIFTEEN

Friday, August 2

*W*e found out in the morning at breakfast that the city was at an elevation of 7,000-plus feet, where the oxygen level is low. At home, our elevation is 825 feet. I asked Tom if he was okay to continue the trip. He replied, "It's like being in a fire. Do you stay and get burned up or get the heck out of the fire?"

Departure time was 6:52 am, and we were greeted with a beautiful sunrise and a cool temperature of 63 degrees. While getting fuel for Abigail a short distance down the road, Tom helped a lady who was having difficulty getting the machine to start working the pump. That was a good sign to me that he was recovered.

A quote from Tom Dapp, a Model A Club member, for the day: "Every 1,000 feet of elevation equals 10 percent less power of the Model A engine." Abajo Peak, at 11,360 feet, was off to our west. Dry Wash National Forest loomed in the distance. A road sign read, "Cabinets and Headstones." Horses grazing were a common sight now. Thoughts and emotions jumped inside our heads today. Would we make our goal? Anything could happen that could hinder us from accomplishing it.

Feelings darted from euphoria to resignation. Keeping the car going forward was all we needed to do. Utah is not laced with an abundance of roads, especially super-highways in the southeastern part of the state. Our roads today were state highways that twisted and roller-coasted their way through the canyons and mountains. A 6 percent downgrade felt like a good toboggan ride. Straight down. Whoopee!

Landscapes of Utah.

This area of Utah is sought out for rock climbing, camping, horseback riding, stargazing, mountain biking, running, river rafting, ATV safaris, hunting for lizards, fishing, birdwatching, and exploring the impressive monuments. Route 191 took us through the Navajo Indian reservation to Route 160, where we turned east to the Four Corners.

Abigail made it to New Mexico.

Ninety-two miles after leaving Monticello, we arrived at the Four Corners Monument at 9:45 am. The trip to this point had not been easy. But we made it! Abigail had been driven to all the lower forty-eight states.

The drive to the Four Corners monument is an out-of-the-way trip for most travelers, but it was a quick way for us to reach the two states we needed to complete our quest and the only spot in the United States where four states come together. The monument marks the exact spot where the four states meet, Colorado, Utah, New Mexico and Arizona.

Arriving at Four Corners.

The Four Corners monument has been included in modern high accuracy Global Positioning System (GPS) geodetic surveys, producing three-dimensional coordinates accurate to an inch or better.[15] The monument itself is a bronze disk embedded in granite.

---

[15] 15 Google. Four Corners Monument.

Tom and Sharon standing in four states:
Arizona, New Mexico, Utah, and Colorado.

Yes, like good tourists, we had our photo taken there. Younger visitors did handstands on the spot. A couple from Ireland chatted with us while we were souvenir shopping for handmade Navajo jewelry. Although the Four Corners Monument is in a desolate desert area, there are nearby (250-plus miles) attractions, such as the Grand Canyon-North Park in Arizona, and Mesa Verde National Park in Mancos, Colorado. The area is filled with archaeological sites, remote landscapes, and scenic byways.

Abigail leaving Four Corners.

At this point, euphoria would best describe our mood. If we could do cartwheels to celebrate, we would have! Indeed, it was a celebration and a relief to have accomplished our goal. We had made it over the mountains and across deserts! Yes, we made it, we made it, we made it! Sometimes it is still hard to believe that we did drive Abigail in all the lower forty-eight states. Now it did not matter what happened to us. The car could break down and need to be trailered home, but no one could take away our accomplishment! Before we left Four Corners, we shared our accomplishment with our Facebook friends.

AAH-OOH GAH! AAH-OOH GAH! S P E C I A L R E P O R T

"WHAT IF ABIGAIL COULD TALK?"

Abigail here. If only I could talk, I would say how honored I am to have been chosen to do this awesome trip! Just think, eighty-nine-year-old little me has been in forty-eight states and the District of Columbia. How many other eighty-nine-year-old cars can say that? Not many— maybe none. Henry Ford said, "You can't build a reputation on what you are going to do." [16]

I'm calling Tom and Sharon my dad and mom, even though they are younger than me, because they take care of me. Tom tucks me in my little garage each night at home and sees that I have all the oil and gas I need. He polishes me and pays attention to any little noise that I make and fixes me.

This has been a tough trip for me—so many mountains, so many ups and downs. Sometimes I needed more oxygen too.

All along the way, I held my head up high and rode out the miles with the sixteen-wheelers, motorcycles, and Broncos. I absolutely agree with the answer Henry Ford proposed people would reply to him when he asked, "What they wanted was "faster horses."[17] I sure could have used more and faster horses under my hood many times on this trip. Remember, I only have forty horses!

---

[16] Google. Henry Ford Quotes.

[17] Google. Henry Ford Quotes.

I think back to another awesome trip I made with Sharon and Tom, the "Pikes Peak or Bust" tour sponsored by MAFCA in 2005. Pikes Peak is the highest summit of the southern front range of the Rocky Mountains in North America. The ultra-prominent 14,115-foot four-teener is in Pike National Forest, twelve miles west of downtown Colorado Springs, Colorado. The mountain is named in honor of American explorer Zebulon Pike.[18] Katherine Lee Bates stood on the top of Pikes Peak for just thirty minutes in the summer of 1893, but that was all the inspiration she needed to write a patriotic poem called "America." She was impressed with the beauty and vastness of the United States and was inspired to write the words during a 2,000-mile cross country train trip. And, as I was parked on the top of Pikes Peak, surrounded by the "spacious skies," I saw the "amber waves of grain" and was awestruck by the "purple mountains' majesty"—"America the Beautiful"[19] was played via loudspeakers at the summit.

I've had many other memorable experiences. I've ridden in Fourth of July parades, Veteran's Day parades, city festival parades and participated in nursing home visitations, and weddings. My favorite wedding ride was for Sharon and Tom's grandson Anthony and his bride Leslie. So, you see, my life has been full and satisfying, and I look forward to many more fun trips.

---

[18] Google. Pikes Peak.

[19] Google: America the Beautiful"

Grandson Anthony Laupp and his bride, Leslie,
on their wedding day, April 28, 2012.

Continuing Day Fifteen:

By 11:00 am, we were heading home. Yay! To avoid traveling through the Rocky Mountains, we chose to take a
more southern route around the edge of the mountains
in New Mexico and Colorado. At one point, we thought
we would reverse our route north then turn east at Salt
Lake City. But that would have meant another two-day

trip up Utah. For me, the trip down Utah (heading south) was a onetime event. So, our new plan was to take 160 to 64 east to Farmington, New Mexico. A straight stretch of road was ahead; we were more than happy to take it!

By this time, we had been on the road for two weeks. To finish our trip home, we were taking the route with the least high elevations. I was so glad for that. We had had enough stress and anxiety the previous night with our breathing problems. Leaving the Ute Mountain and Navajo Indian Reservations near Farmington, we wondered, "Could we have given them any worse lands?" As soon as we exited these areas, the grass was lush and green, trees were more plentiful, and there were fewer desert conditions.

In Farmington, a Native American man parked next to us at McDonald's where we stopped for lunch. He looked to be the grandfather—not the father—of three elementary school-aged children. He told us, "I would like to take a senior trip, but I am worried about the children. I worry about everything."

For many of the people living in this area, owning a car like ours (even though ours is not a show car) or taking a trip like ours would probably never be possible for them. "Lord, we are thankful for our gifts and opportunities."

Sometimes one wonders why specific people enter our life's path. What could we say to that man? How could we serve him? He must have needed us in his life that day. There is a divine plan for everything. So, we just listened and showed him respect and concern and tried to reach out to him with God's love that was in our hearts.

Leaving Farmington, we were more relaxed, having accomplished our goal and traveling on less mountainous roads. Alleluia! There was one lane of city traffic in Farmington because of sewer repairs. We spotted Laundratopia, a huge laundromat, and we could smell the soap. There was also, a huge flea market along the highway with colorful umbrellas at each table. Remember the three crosses that would dot the countryside for so many years, not many of which remain? A surviving set of three crosses was on our left just after we passed a Navajo Indian school.

A dump truck driver gave us a "love toot" as he passed us. His passing scared me. Tom knew he was coming, but I couldn't see much out my side mirror. Sometimes I would see the vehicle's reflection in the front window before it passed us. Wouldn't you know, an opposite reaction by an unhappy motorist happened shortly after the happy toot. This fellow blew his horn and sped extremely fast around us; unhappy we were on the road. What was his problem?! He zoomed around several more cars in front of us. That was our only negative response to our eighty-nine-year-old car being on the road for the entire trip! As we traveled forward, we passed many large areas of trailers and mobile homes, each with their own personal "graveyard" of cars, trucks, etc. I thought to myself, *I've been in the car long enough today. My knees and elbows are tired of being bent and flexed for so many hours.*

We had climbed back to 7,000 feet from 5,000 feet at Four Corners. Approaching the Apache reservation, we saw lightning and threatening looking skies. Our cheeks were pink and warm as it was 89 degrees inside the car and 95 degrees outside. We had a device in the car that reported the interior car temperature as well as the outside air temperature.

The Continental Divide is at 7,380 feet. The watershed from this area flows into the Rio Grande River. The terrain is desolate with huge rock cliffs. A sudden steep downhill in the road surprised us, and pouring rain was ahead. When the rain came, a fragrant pine scent delighted us. Soon we were in the middle of a lightning storm, with the temperature having decreased to 81/75 (inside/outside). It rained so hard that many drivers pulled off the road.

The rain was gone at 6,475 feet but not the wind. Tom drove us through a 5 percent downgrade wonderfully. We were hoping our destination city that day would be at an elevation of 4,000 to 5,000 feet. The color of the homes was sand-red to brown on both the roofs and bodies of the houses. This coloring made the structures blend in with the surroundings. The stores we frequently saw were Family Dollar, Wells Fargo, Subway, and McDonald's.

Rain was back and pounding down harder as we ended our day. Tom was using his ever-so-powerful six-inch windshield wiper! A caution sign read: "When Light Flashing-Wildlife is Detected."

Rio Rancho, New Mexico, turned out to be our landing spot for the day. After not finding a room at two motels, the Days Inn vacancy was welcomed by us. Today's mileage was 347.4 miles and a total trip mileage of

4,490 miles. The check in staff took our picture holding a map of the United States to memorialize the completion of our traveling to all the lower forty-eight states, including the newly-added eight states.

Tom and Sharon holding map of all forty-eight states and the District of Columbia that they have driven Abigail in.

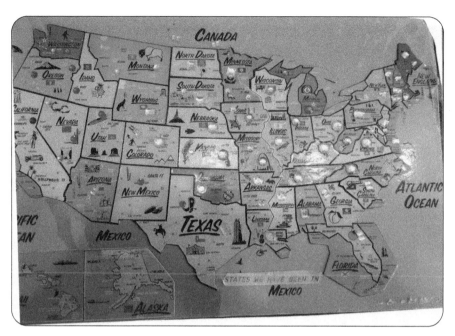

Map of USA

DAY SIXTEEN

Saturday, August 3

A sunny day and a mild 71 degrees greeted us at 6:42 am as we left the Days Inn. Thankfully, we were at 5,000 feet in Rio Rancho and did not experience any breathing problems. Our trip today eventually pointed northeast. The car started right up thanks to Tom putting a large plastic bag over the engine and under the hood because there had been a rainstorm the previous night.

Heading southeast on Highway 550 out of Rio Rancho, we gassed up for the first time of the day. Our emotions remained celebratory and incredulous that we had accomplished our goal. We were riding at the top of the mountain, and it felt good! We said a prayer together: "Thank you, Lord, for this day and being on our way home."

Our travel time was now sixteen days. Tom said, "Abigail has not dumped oil out of the motor this trip." Soon we were traveling northeast on Interstate 25. The ups and downs, sometimes just a few hundred feet, often resulted in steep climbs and descents.

If you lived in New Mexico, you would learn a lot of new names, especially city names. Tom said, "You have to be careful how you say them." Ha! Ha! If you are interested, we passed an area of 5,400 acres for sale.

A climb to 6,296 feet took us immediately back down to an ear-popping descent. There were railroad tracks in the median between the north and southbound roads. This area of New Mexico abounds with Indian reservations: Sandia, Santa Ana, Santo Domingo, Cochiti, Tesuque, San Felipe, and many others. At 6,870 feet, Tom commented that the wind was terrible. In the middle of nowhere and at 7,122 feet, a hitchhiker appeared on our side of the road. He was an older fellow with grey hair and a winter coat. I wondered if anybody missed him. The houses were almost hiding in the landscape and were not taller than the small trees and shrubs surrounding them. Apache Canyon was next on our path, with a quick descent and immediate climb back to 7,241 feet. Five motorcyclists passed us with the last one waving to us. At this point, we were traveling through the Santa Fe National Forest and could smell the pine trees. The temperature dropped to 75 degrees.

It seemed like we had been driving for a long time, but it was only 9:05 am when we gassed up at a Speedway station. Abigail had used six gallons for the last 112 miles. The steep climbs had been hard work for poor little Abigail! Still on Interstate 25, we passed Romeroville, Las Vegas (New Mexico), and the Santa Fe Trail. One of the few sheriff deputies we had seen on this trip was parked on our side of the highway. But he was not getting us!

This area had more grasslands, cattle, and Russian olive trees. Today felt like a nice summer day with low humidity and no sweating—yet. The same five motorcyclists passed us again, and each one of them waved this time. Guess we were bonding with them! When you are on a trip like this, it doesn't take much to connect with others. It was only 9:49 am, and we were taking our second chocolate break of the day.

The Canadian River and Kiowa National Grasslands were to our right and the Turkey Mountains to the left. By 10:45 am, it was getting warmer, up to 93 degrees. We had all the windows open now. The Philmont Boy Scout Ranch is in this area. As a youngster, Tom took the train from Milwaukee, Wisconsin, to the ranch with members of his Troop 399. He was there for a week and earned scout badges.

We thought we would play our music CDs all along this trip, but we did not. It was too windy to hear any music or the radio. We only listened to Handel's Messiah on Sundays for our church time, and that was earlier in the day before all the windows were open.

Just before noon, we stopped for lunch at McDonald's in Raton, New Mexico, and now we were only miles from Colorado and one more state closer to home. This McDonald's was packed to the gills with patrons, so we could not hurry if we wanted to. We met a lady from Texas. She had her English cream golden retriever in her car, and they were on their way home. She was another person who gushed all over the car and wished she had one and could take a trip like ours. Again, could she ever do that? Probably not, but we did not want to discourage her. We talked "dogs" for a while then parted ways. She was one of our blessings on this trip.

Immediately upon entering Colorado, we were on a climb in the Rockies but still on the Santa Fe Trail. Fishers Peak was on our right with an elevation of 9,827 feet. Then we passed through Trinidad, Walsenburg, and Pueblo. Pueblo looks like the America we know—grass, homes with trees, and lots of corporate buildings. For a third time, we were passed on the road by the five motorcyclists, who all waved and gave us thumbs up. One bike was orange with a stuffed gorilla on the backseat. The outside temperature was still 93 degrees, and the interior of the car was 83 degrees. Approaching Colorado Springs, we passed Pikes Peak International Raceway, Cheyenne Mountain State Park, and Pikes Peak. Motel rooms in Colorado Springs were hard to find. After three attempts, we finally found one for $200, Townplace Suites by Marriott. Today's mileage was 372 miles, and total trip mileage was 4,791.6.

DAY SEVENTEEN

Sunday, August 4

*W*e were leaving Colorado Springs on a sunny, 69-degree day, no jackets required. There were 1,165 miles to home. Our elevation the previous night was 6,031 feet, and both of us had had some breathing issues. We would be glad to be home at our familiar 825 feet of elevation.

By 6:46 am, we were rolling east on Highway 24 with a lower speed limit of only 55 mph. By 7:09 am, we were out of the rat race of traffic in Colorado Springs and back in country settings the likes of which are found in Indiana. The electrical and phone lines strung between poles looked like crystals in the sunshine. Cattle, including longhorns, were grazing on the hillsides. We passed the second windmill farm of the day and very few houses. An hour and a half later, we stopped at a Sinclair station for a gas and bathroom break. Keeping to our tradition of taking home a beef jerky stick for the dogs when we return from road trips, we purchased two sticks and a Colorado T-shirt as a souvenir.

We turned north on Colorado State road 71 to the town of Last Chance and headed east again. A common sign on both highways, SR 71 and Colorado State Road 36, was, "WARNING: No Snow Plowing This Road 7P-5A."

Oops—a small, little critter ran in front of us, but he made it safely across the road.

A message from Barb said, "Everything good at home, and it was a nice day." The town of Cope, at an elevation of 4,419 feet, had a picnic table for travelers. Our elevations were slowly decreasing. The town of Idalia was sitting at 3,960 feet. The local gas station had no gas, even though the sign read, "Open 24/7 with Credit Card." Now just twenty-nine miles to the Colorado border, we would be one more state closer to home.

At our last turn, a lady had been hitchhiking, carrying five bags and a suitcase and talking on her phone. There was no room in our car as we were packed to the brim. At 10:45 am, we rode into the Central time zone and lost an hour on the clock.

We crossed the Kansas border at 10:50 am. This was going to be a long ride as Kansas is 410 miles wide. The wind was extremely strong, making our things fly around in the backseat. It was time to close my window because the window was facing south, the direction of the wind. Oil wells, corn, and wheat fields were plentiful. The "Majestic Services" gas station in St. Francis was our lunch and gas break. Steve Brigham, Jr., this stop is for you because you said it is your stop on the treks you make across the country. Steve Jr. is the son of our car club friend Steve Sr. He is a long-distance trucker. The Subway restaurant here was packed full of Sunday churchgoers dressed in their best clothes. A motorcycle museum was also located on the property. The Republican River was nearby. So far, we had traveled 221 miles for the day and had 921 miles to home.

At McDonald (the town), the elevation was 3,389 feet, and the temperature was 97 degrees. By 1:30 pm, we were unbelievably hot and just enduring and hanging in for one more hour; then we would call it a day. After another gas and bathroom stop in Norton, we stopped to see if a motorcyclist who had pulled over to the side of the road needed help. He said, no—he was just changing his shirt because he was burning up.

Phillipsburg was our overnight stay. Total mileage: 5,160.4 and 345 miles for the day.

DAY EIGHTEEN

Monday, August 5

An early start in the dark at 6:30 am was short-lived. Abigail would not start. Tom was exasperated! Harry, the motel owner, knew the owner of the next-door Chrysler dealership. Maybe he could help, but the shop did not open until 8:00 am. Tom continued to troubleshoot until two minutes until eight, when he walked to the dealership. The fellows there knew an expert on Model A's. They gave him a call, and he said he would be over within the hour.

His name was Ron Kester, and he and Tom determined that the ignition switch and cable needed to be replaced. Now this was another situation in which we were so blessed. We couldn't have stopped at a better place to receive help. It was not luck or chance; it was divine providence and our heavenly Father watching over us. We were in the hinterlands of Kansas, far away from any big city with vast supplies of almost anything a person might need. But it turns out that Ron had a Model A restoration business, and his daughter had taken it over when he retired. And the store, with all the parts we needed, was only five miles away! After the switch and cable were replaced, the car started right up, and we had more people in our lives to be thankful for.

L-R, Tom Laupp, Chrysler mechanic, and Ron Kester looking satisfied after fixing Abigail.

"On the Road Again" was the song we hummed at 11:00 am. Even though we were in lower altitudes—1,791 feet—we were on high ground and could see for miles all around. At 12:05 pm, we drove through Belleville and reminisced of a former trip when we spent the night there and had to replace our muffler. The night we stayed there had a severe storm with hail and tornado warnings. The motel owner had arranged for us to park Abigail under the next-door bank's canopy to avoid storm damage. Doesn't it seem like we've always been taken care of?

We were traveling on parts of the historic "Pony Express Auto Tour Route." While Tom was driving, I was multi-tasking—texting friends and family, making our daily notes, map reading, attending to some dog club business, helping Tom watch the road, and getting out snacks and cooling neck packs. Now instead of mountains, we had vast fields of corn and windmill farms. A man pedaling on a recumbent bicycle was making upward progress. I wondered what his destination was. I didn't see many flower beds at the houses we were passing and wondered how mine were doing— probably looking for a big dose of Miracle-Gro.

We stopped at Casey's for gas and the bathroom. Huge herds of cattle were grazing in fields on both sides of the highway. An asphalt plant on the right had flames spewing from a large pipe. Oh! Two large curves and a long down-hill came into sight. Usually, the road had been as straight an arrow. We ended our day in St. Joseph, Missouri, at the Quality Inn with supper at the Cracker Barrel.

Total trip miles were 5,412. Today's miles were only 252, but remember, we had a late start.

DAY NINETEEN

Tuesday, August 6

At 6:42 am on a humid 74-degree and partly sunny day, everything was packed orderly in the car, and we were leaving St. Joseph, Missouri, and the Quality Inn. Or so we thought. The car would not start! Within fifteen minutes, that "good old Tom" got her started, and we were rolling again. Tom said, "I'm so tired of this car."

Traveling east on Route 36, the road was hilly with an abundance of trees on both sides. At this point, the road was a four-lane divided highway. Today should be our last full day of traveling; the next day would be a short day. Tom was so happy. We could both see the end of this trip. That was a cause for happiness!

*Frequent event! Abigail needed to be filled up every
150 Miles, totaling 40 gas stops for the trip.*

Wind farms were a frequent sight on the entire trip and
didn't disappoint today; all the blades were turning. By
7:46 am, we had been on the road for one hour and fifty-six minutes. Passing a long tanker going uphill was a
blast. Hannibal, Missouri, was our entry point into Illinois
and Interstate 72. Hannibal was Mark Twain's boyhood
home. Halfway across the Mississippi was Illinois. Now
we were sailing. The next state was Indiana.

Oh, if only we could hop right over to home. It would take us the remainder of this day and part of the next to get there. Remember that Illinois was our home for nineteen years, and we are familiar with most areas of the state. So, as we started traveling on I-72, we realized how close to Interstates 55 and 57 we would be. Those highways would take us to where we formerly lived. But, Tom said, "No, we are not stopping in Bloomington." He said he'd had it. He had also said he was done three days before. For the record, I was done too. Tom further said, "I can take the car (Chrysler) that has been in the garage at home for the last few weeks and go back to Illinois and see our friends." So, I didn't ask again.

It was just before nine o'clock when we opened the front window to the middle notch. That helps cool down our feet and legs, which were fried by the afternoon. Blue corn flowers blew gently in the ditches alongside the road. We took advantage of a gas pump with no building to fill up. It took credit cards 24/7. Barb Myers called with a message, saying, "Everything good at home." I appreciated her daily updates.

The presence of many creeks and rivers contributed to a greener landscape than we had observed in the more western states. A huge American flag flew at half-mast because of mass shootings in Texas and Ohio.

Woohoo—we passed a car on an uphill. That was the third vehicle we'd passed on this trip, and two had been uphill. Drinking water frequently to keep hydrated was still one of our daily goals. The car we passed up eventually perked up enough to pass us. I was waiting to get to my spot of earthly heaven—Andrews, Indiana. I was sure Tom was too. You know what I like to eat from gas stations? Egg salad sandwiches. They are so good. We thought that maybe we would stop at Casey's for lunch, in which case, I would get one.

We were making progress. At 9:46 am, we passed around Shelbyville and a junkyard full of classic cars. Their bodies were colorful and looked in good condition. Today, in contrast to prior days on this trip, it was hard for both of us to keep awake. Gum, music, soda, and chocolate were helping.

We traveled for a while on the Abraham Lincoln National Heritage Trail. Remember the old Burma Shave ads? Here is a sign like those: it read, "My wife is gone, the kids are scared, but I'm prepared. Guns save lives.com."

Along the Illinois River, there are high rock cliffs and bluffs. By 11:16 am, the cities of Winchester, Walnut Creek, Jacksonville, and Beardstown crossed our path. The altitude was a whopping 534 feet! Two hundred fifty-six miles had been added to our trip this morning. There were only 302 miles to the finish line.

Love's gas station did not live up to my expectations— no egg salad sandwiches! Tom and I split a dry ham and cheese sandwich and leftover fruit from the previous night's supper.

Another landmark we noted as we passed by was the 90-degree latitude sign—a quarter way around the world. Other historic highlights at this juncture of our trip included the Abraham Lincoln Presidential Library and Museum, state fairgrounds, Mr. Lincoln's hometown— Springfield, Illinois— Camp Butler, and Camp Butler National Cemetery. Continuing at a low altitude of 510 feet sat the Sangamon River. A familiar spot to us was the city of Decatur and Millikin University. Our children had USA swim meets several times a year at the university.

We stopped at a second Love's Truck Stop so Tom could make an adjustment under the hood. Three fellows from the garage ran out to see our car. They got right under the hood with Tom. They were impressed with our trip as we showed them the map of our 6,000-mile route. One guy said, "I'd never get my wife to do that, especially with no air conditioning!"

Passing through Decatur with its oil wells, I wondered if my friend Kathy still had her oil wells there. Just like at home this time of year, there was a yellow crop duster spraying the fields.

The overnight was spent at the LaQuinta in Champaign, Illinois. The total miles of the day: 381; our total trip miles: 5,800. Miles to HOME: 185.

DAY TWENTY

Wednesday, August 7

$\mathcal{E}$ verything had been packed the previous night, so we were ready for a quick departure from the LaQuinta in Champaign, Illinois. I didn't take any notes that day, just kept praying and keeping my fingers crossed—and anything else that could be crossed—for a safe, trouble-free trip home. Our route was Interstate 57 to State Highway 24 to State Road 105 to Andrews. We reminisced about the past as we traveled through familiar places like Rantoul, Paxton, Gilman, and Watseka in Illinois. But "Back Home in Indiana" played in our minds as we traveled through Kentland, Remington, Monticello, Logansport, and Wabash in Indiana.

At 11:35 am, we arrived home, safe and sound, after a 20-day, 5,985-mile trip. Alleluia, thank you, Lord! Thoughts of rounding out our trip to 6,000 miles briefly crossed our minds. Simultaneously we said to each other, "No, I can't take another mile in this car today!" So be it—5,985 miles it is!

Our average speed during the trip was 49 miles per hour. The average gas mileage was 18 miles per gallon.

Barb had brought the pups back home shortly before we arrived. They and Montana, our kitty, were glad to see us, as we were to see them. I did not forget to give them their beef jerky stick purchased so many miles ago in Colorado.

What's next? Drive another 30,000 miles to accumulate 300,000 miles driven by us in Abigail!

Sharon happy to be home with Montana (the cat), Patches, and Francis (the Collies).

At home, Tom, happy to say, "We did it!"

BIBLIOGRAPHY

"America the Beautiful." https://en.m.wikipedia.org

California. https://www.ca.gov

Ford, Henry. https://www.goalcast.comt

Four Corners Monument. https://en.m.wikiepdia.org

Frost, Robert 1922. "Stopping by Woods on a Snowy Night." https://en.m.wikipedia.org

Hedglin, Bayley, "Welcome to Juan Country," *Utah's Canyon Country, 2019.*

Idaho. https://idaho.gov

Nevada. https://nv.gov

Oregon. https://oregon.gov

Pikes Peak. https://coloradosprings.gov

Salt Lake Dessert. https://www.americnsouthwest.net

Utah. https://en.m.wikepedia.org

Ute, Native American Tribe. Last updated May 4, 2020. https://attheu.utah.edu

Washington. https://en.m.wikepedia.org